Introduction

Quilting for charities can be very rewarding. There are many worthy and good causes that can benefit from the efforts of quilters. What is truly wonderful about quilting for charities is that you can pick and choose the causes that are near and dear to your heart. *Quick & Easy Charity Quilts* has many quilts with lots of possibilities for both charity quilts and everyday quilts. These patterns are versatile. Pick and choose your patterns and customize them for either your selected charity or as a fun lap quilt for around your home. Whichever you choose to do, you'll find great patterns with lots of style as you turn the pages. Honor a veteran or fallen soldier, support a cancer cause or maybe donate to a nursing home. Whatever your chosen charity, you'll find a great pattern that will be perfect for your cause.

Enjoy!

Table of Contents

Finding a Charity for Your Quilts

There are many reasons to make a charity quilt. Maybe you have a special cause near and dear to your heart. Maybe it's just something you wish to do to pay it forward. Whatever reason you have for wanting to explore charity quilting, you'll find lots of good organizations more than willing to accept your quilts and put them to good use. It's just a matter of finding the right one for your purpose.

Cancers—Probably the most widely available resources for donating quilts are cancer support centers. Cancer seems to touch all our lives. You can probably think of someone you know who has or has had cancer. Most cancer quilts are made and donated to individuals who have cancer and are going through treatment. The quilt gives comfort and warmth to the patient while undergoing chemotherapy. The symbol used for these quilts and the cancers they represent is a ribbon. Each ribbon has an assigned color to represent the particular cancer. Breast cancer is the most widely recognized with pink as its color. Teal is for ovarian cancer, and lavender is used for all cancers.

Alzheimer's—The color most often associated with Alzheimer's disease is purple. Quilts with attachments such as zippers, buttons and ties are sometimes used to keep the patient busy. These are called fidget quilts. They are sometimes weighted to give the patient a secure feeling.

Autism—The symbol often used for autism is a puzzle piece. Colors range from very plain to colorful. As for Alzheimer's, fidget quilts are also used for autism.

Veterans—The quilts used for our veterans are usually patriotic-themed and made in red, white and blue. These quilts are donated to nursing homes, Quilts of Valor and many more organizations you can easily find through internet searches or through your local quilt guilds.

Hospitals—Hospitals are always in need of quilts for the neonatal units, long-term care and outpatient hospice. You can usually find more information at your local hospitals through their health foundation.

Senior Homes—Senior homes are always happy to receive lap quilts for their residents. Call local senior care or living center to see if they require a certain size.

Quilt Guilds—If you are a quilter and wish to donate quilts to a cause, the best place for information on gifting them is your local quilt guild. Attend a meeting or join a guild to find many opportunities to participate in charitable quilting. ●

Charity Symbol Chart

Veterans	All Cancer	Melanoma
Ovarian Cancer	Childhood Cancer	Colon Cancer
Lung Cancer	Prostate Cancer	Leukemia
Breast Cancer	Testicular Cancer	

Simple Simon

This quick and easy quilt would make the perfect choice for any military charity group or nursing home, or with the right fabric choices, it would make a great children's quilt. It's very versatile.

Design by Karen DuMont of KariePatch Designs
Quilted by The Longarm Network

Skill Level
Beginner

Finished Size
Quilt Size: 50" x 47"
Block Size: 7" x 6"
Number of Blocks: 18

Materials
- ⅓ yard white solid
- ½ yard red, white and blue stripe
- 1⅛ yards red print
- 1⅜ yards dark blue print
- Backing to size
- Batting to size
- Thread
- Basic sewing tools and supplies

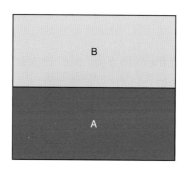

Simple Simon
7" x 6" Finished Block
Make 18

Project Notes
Read all instructions before beginning this project.

Stitch right sides together using a ¼" seam allowance unless otherwise specified.

Materials and cutting lists assume 40" of usable fabric width for yardage.

Cutting

From white solid:
- Cut 4 (2" by fabric width) D/E strips.

From red, white and blue stripe:
- Cut 4 (3½" by fabric width) strips.
  Subcut strips into 18 (3½" x 7½") B rectangles.

From red print:
- Cut 4 (3½" by fabric width) strips.
- Subcut strips into 18 (3½" x 7½") A rectangles.
- Cut 6 (2¼" by fabric width) binding strips.

From dark blue print:
- Cut 3 (6½" by fabric width) strips.
  Subcut strips into 18 (6½") C squares.
- Cut 5 (4½" by fabric width) F/G strips.

Completing the Blocks

1. Referring to the block drawing, sew A to B on the long sides to make a Simple Simon block; press. Repeat to make a total of 18 Simple Simon blocks.

Completing the Quilt

Refer to the Assembly Diagram for construction steps as needed.

1. Referring to Figure 1, arrange and sew a C square on one short side of a Simple Simon block to make an A-B-C unit; press. Repeat to make 18 A-B-C units.

A-B-C Unit
Make 18

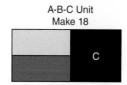

Figure 1

2. Sew three A-B-C units together to complete a block row; press. Repeat to make a total of six rows.

3. Arrange the block rows and sew together to complete the quilt center; press.

4. Sew D/E strips together on the short ends to make one long strip; press. Subcut strip into two each 2" x 36½" D and 2" x 42½" E strips.

This same pattern could easily be done in fun novelty fabrics for a young child. This pattern has many options if you use your imagination.

5. Sew D strips to opposite sides of the quilt center and E strips to the top and bottom; press.

6. Sew F/G strips together on the short ends to make one long strip; press. Subcut strip into two each 4½" x 39½" F and 4½" x 50½" G strips.

7. Sew F strips to opposite sides of the quilt center and G strips to the top and bottom to complete the quilt top; press.

8. Layer, quilt as desired and bind referring to Quilting Basics on page 47. Sample quilt was machine-quilted with an edge-to-edge patriotic stars pattern. ●

Inspiration

"I'm donating this quilt to the Veterans Affairs Hospital in Richmond, Va. I belong to three guilds that make and donate quilts to local children's hospitals, veteran's organizations and churches that give quilts to those in need." —Karen DuMont

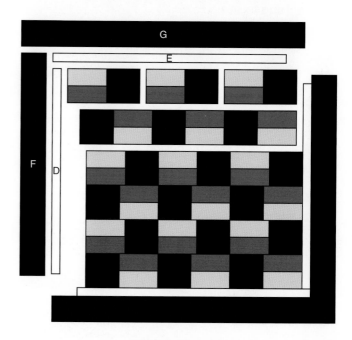

Simple Simon
Assembly Diagram 50" x 47"

Neo-Preemie Quilt

This easy block quilt is the perfect size to use in the neo-natal unit at your local hospital. It could also be used as a mat for any newborn baby.

Designed & Quilted by Carolyn S. Vagts

Skill Level
Beginner

Finished Size
Quilt Size: 24" x 24"
Block Size: 12" x 12"
Number of Blocks: 4

Materials
- 1 fat quarter each of medium and dark blue prints
- ⅓ yard light blue print
- ⅝ yard white tonal
- Backing to size
- Batting to size
- Thread
- Basic sewing tools and supplies

Project Notes
Read all instructions before beginning this project.

Stitch right sides together using a ¼" seam allowance unless otherwise specified.

Materials and cutting lists assume 40" of usable fabric width for yardage and 20" for fat quarters.

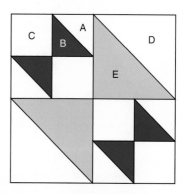

Triple Bow
12" x 12" Finished Block
Make 4

Cutting

From medium blue print fat quarter:
- Cut 4 (6⅞") squares.
    Subcut each square in half on 1 diagonal to make 8 E triangles.

From dark blue print fat quarter:
- Cut 8 (3⅞") squares.
    Subcut each square in half on 1 diagonal to make 16 B triangles.

From light blue print:
- Cut 3 (2¼" by fabric width) binding strips.

From white tonal:

- Cut 1 (6⅞" by fabric width) strip.
  Subcut strip into 4 (6⅞") squares, cut each square in half on 1 diagonal to make 8 D triangles.
- Cut 1 (3⅞" by fabric width) strip.
  Subcut strip into 8 (3⅞") squares; cut each square in half on 1 diagonal to make 16 A triangles.
- Cut 2 (3½" by fabric width) strips.
  Subcut strips into 16 (3½") C squares.

Completing the Blocks

1. Arrange and stitch an A and B triangle together as shown in Figure 1 to make an A-B unit; press. Repeat to make a total of 16 A-B units.

A-B Unit
Make 16

Figure 1

2. Referring to Figure 2, sew a C square on one side of an A-B unit to make an A-B-C unit; press. Repeat to make a total of 16 A-B-C units.

A-B-C Unit
Make 16

Figure 2

3. Arrange and stitch two A-B-C units together as shown in Figure 3 to make a four-patch unit; press. Repeat to make a total of eight four-patch units.

Four-Patch Unit
Make 8

Figure 3

4. Referring to Figure 4, arrange and stitch one each D and E triangle together to make a D-E unit; press. Repeat to make a total of eight D-E units.

D-E Unit
Make 8

Figure 4

5. Arrange two each four-patch units and D-E units into two rows as shown in Figure 5. Sew units into rows and stitch rows together to complete one Triple Bow block; press. Repeat to make a total of four blocks.

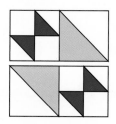

Figure 5

Completing the Quilt

1. Referring to the Assembly Diagram, arrange the four blocks into two rows of two blocks each. Sew the blocks into rows and join the rows to complete the quilt top; press.

2. Layer, quilt as desired and bind referring to Quilting Basics on page 47. Sample quilt was machine-quilted with an edge-to-edge meander. ●

Inspiration

"I'll be donating my quilts to the neonatal unit at St. Francis Hospital in Indianapolis, Ind. Check your local hospital if you would like to donate in your own community."
—Carolyn S. Vagts

Neo-Preemie Quilt
Assembly Diagram 24" x 24"

This easy quilt pattern could be made gender specific or even with scraps. The choice is yours.

Patriotic Star

The large blocks in this quilt make it a quick but lovely option for displaying patriotism. It would also look wonderful in fabrics of your own choosing.

Designed & Quilted by Holly Daniels

Skill Level
Confident Beginner

Finished Size
Quilt Size: 64" x 56"
Block Size: 20" x 16" and 20" x 20"
Number of Blocks: 4 and 4

Materials
- 1⅛ yards red tonal
- 1¾ yards white solid
- 2 yards blue tonal
- Backing to size
- Batting to size
- Thread
- Basic sewing tools and supplies

Project Notes
Read all instructions before beginning this project.

Stitch right sides together using a ¼" seam allowance unless otherwise specified.

Materials and cutting lists assume 40" of usable fabric width for yardage.

Cutting

From red tonal:
- Cut 1 (8⅞" by fabric width) strip.
  Subcut strip into 4 (8⅞") B squares.
- Cut 2 (11⅞" by fabric width) strips.
  Subcut strips into 4 (11⅞") F squares.

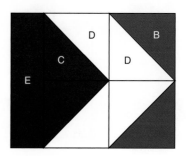

Side
20" x 16" Finished Block
Make 4

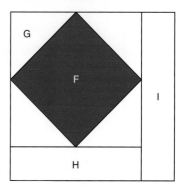

Corner
20" x 20" Finished Block
Make 4

From white solid:
- Cut 4 (8⅞" by fabric width) strips.
  Subcut strips into 16 (8⅞") squares. Label 8 squares as D. Cut the remaining 8 squares in half on 1 diagonal to make 16 G triangles.
- Cut 4 (4½" by fabric width) strips.
  Subcut strips into 4 each 4½" x 16½" H and 4½" x 20½" I rectangles.

From blue tonal:

- Cut 1 (8⅞" by fabric width) strip.
  Subcut strip into 4 (8⅞") C squares.
- Cut 1 (16½" by fabric width) strip.
  Subcut strip into 1 (16½") A square and
  4 (4½" x 16½") E rectangles.
- Cut 3 (4½" by fabric width) J strips.
- Cut 7 (2¼" by fabric width) binding strips.

Completing the Blocks

1. Draw a diagonal line from corner to corner on the wrong side of each D square.

2. With right sides together, pair a B and D square and stitch ¼" on each side of the drawn line as shown in Figure 1. Cut on the drawn line to make two B-D units; press. Trim unit, if needed, to 8½" square. Repeat to make a total of eight B-D units.

Figure 1

3. Repeat step 2 with four each C and D squares to make a total of eight C-D units, again referring to Figure 1.

4. Referring to Figure 2, arrange and sew two B-D units together to make a vertical row. Join two C-D units to make a second vertical row. Sew rows together; press. Trim unit, if needed, to measure 16½" square.

Figure 2

5. Referring to the Side block drawing, arrange and stitch an E rectangle to the C side of the unit made in step 4; press.

6. Repeat steps 4 and 5 to make a total of four Side blocks.

7. Sew two G triangles on opposite sides of an F square as shown in Figure 3; press. Sew two G triangles on the remaining two sides to make an F-G unit; press. Trim unit, if needed, to measure 16½" square. Repeat to make a total of four F-G units; press.

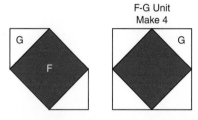

Figure 3

8. Referring to Figure 4, sew an H rectangle to one side of an F-G unit and an I rectangle to an adjacent side to complete one Corner block; press. Repeat to make a total of four Corner blocks.

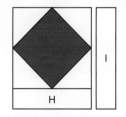

Figure 4

Completing the Quilt

1. Referring to the Assembly Diagram, arrange Corner blocks, Side blocks and the A square into three rows. Sew into rows; press. Sew the rows together to complete the quilt center; press.

2. Sew J strips together on the short ends to make one long strip; press. Subcut strip into two 4½" x 56½" J strips.

3. Sew J strips to opposite sides of the quilt center to complete the quilt top; press.

4. Layer, quilt as desired and bind referring to Quilting Basics on page 47. Sample quilt was custom-quilted with star-themed designs and straight-line quilting. ●

Inspiration

"I have wanted to stitch a Quilt of Valor quilt for a while, and that is where this quilt will eventually go. The center of the quilt is large and makes a nice background for appliqué letters or photos if desired to make it into a presentation quilt. If donating to the Quilts of Valor, check their website for size requirements and local groups." —Holly Daniels

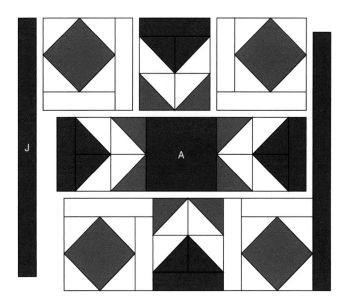

Patriotic Star
Assembly Diagram 64" x 56"

Another option for everyday use for this pattern is to consider it when you need a quick gift or a weekend project. It will work just as well for either.

Sassy Sally

The simple blocks and the size make this pattern the perfect choice for both a scrappy quilt and one for charity-themed use.

Design by Karen DuMont of KariePatch Designs
Quilted by The Longarm Network

Skill Level
Beginner

Finished Size
Quilt Size: 55½" x 63"
Block Size: 8½" x 12½"
Number of Blocks: 20

Materials
- 20 (6½" x 10½") A rectangles in assorted pink fabrics
- ½ yard pink dot
- ⅝ yard pink floral
- 2⅓ yards white tonal
- Backing to size
- Batting to size
- Thread
- Basic sewing tools and supplies

Project Notes
Read all instructions before beginning this project.

Stitch right sides together using a ¼" seam allowance unless otherwise specified.

Materials and cutting lists assume 40" of usable fabric width for yardage.

Cutting

From pink dot:
- Cut 5 (2½" by fabric width) D/E strips.

From pink floral:
- Cut 7 (2¼" by fabric width) binding strips.

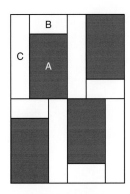

Sassy Sally
8½" x 12½" Finished Block
Make 20

From white tonal:
- Cut 6 (5" by fabric width) F/G strips.
- Cut 20 (2" by fabric width) strips.
  Subcut strips into 40 each 2" x 6½" B and 2" x 13½" C strips.

Completing the Blocks

1. Arrange and stitch B strips on opposite short ends of an A rectangle as shown in Figure 1 to make an A-B unit; press.

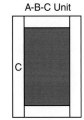

Figure 1

Figure 2

2. Referring to Figure 2, sew C strips on opposite long sides of an A-B unit to make an A-B-C unit; press.

3. Cut the A-B-C unit in half both horizontally and vertically as shown in Figure 3 to make four 4¾" x 6¾" quarter sections.

Quarter Sections

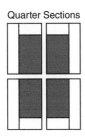

Figure 3

4. Swap the upper right and bottom left quarter sections as shown in Figure 4 and sew quarter sections together into two rows; press. Join rows to complete one Sassy Sally block; press.

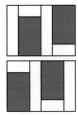

Figure 4

5. Repeat steps 1–4 to make a total of 20 Sassy Sally blocks.

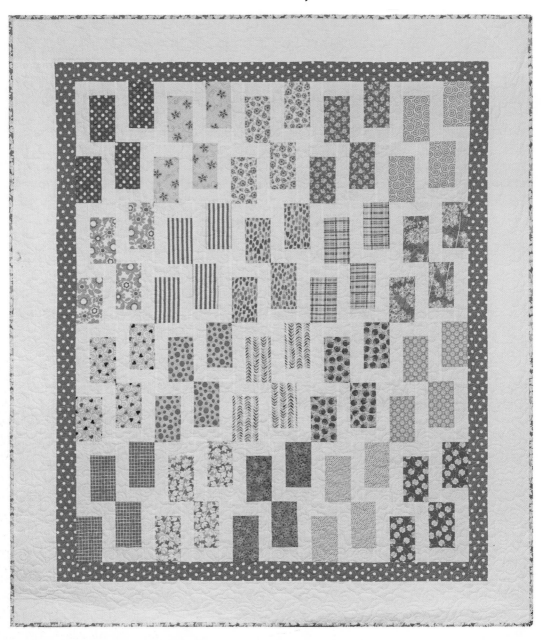

Completing the Quilt

1. Referring to the Assembly Diagram, arrange the blocks into four rows of five blocks each. Sew the blocks together into rows; press. Sew the rows together to complete the quilt center; press.

2. Sew D/E strips together on the short ends to make one long strip; press. Subcut strip into two each 2" x 50½" D and 2" x 47" E strips.

3. Sew D strips to opposite sides of the quilt center and E strips to the top and bottom; press.

4. Sew F/G strips together on the short ends to make one long strip; press. Subcut strip into two each 5" x 54½" F and 5" x 56" G strips.

5. Sew F strips to opposite sides of the quilt center and G strips to the top and bottom to complete the quilt top; press.

6. Layer, quilt as desired and bind referring to Quilting Basics on page 47. Sample quilt was machine-quilted with an edge-to-edge floral swirl pattern. ●

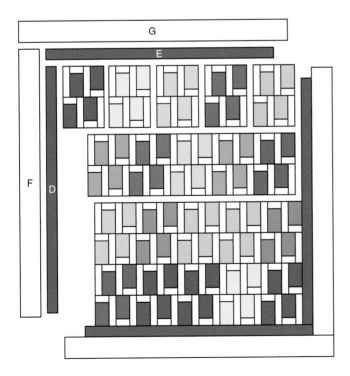

Sassy Sally
Assembly Diagram 55½" x 63"

Inspiration

"I'm donating this quilt to a young mother who is suffering from breast cancer. My daughter-in-law, Bridget, is an 11-year survivor and helps counsel others who suffer from this disease. Bridget has her own charity, Bridget's Brigade, that raises more than $100,000 each year. A percentage is given to the American Cancer Society for research and more than half goes to individual families to help alleviate everyday expenses when going through treatment." —Karen DuMont

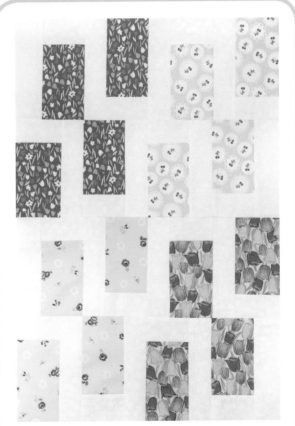

If you are looking for a great pattern that will use up small amounts of fabric or possibly fat quarters to make a very special quilt for someone, this may be just what you're looking for. It has many possibilities.

Foundations

These rectangular bull's-eye blocks are fun to make, and the setting is perfect for multiple quilters to work on. Use this pattern to make quilts for charity or for your home.

Design by Lyn Brown
Quilted by Cathy O'Brien

Skill Level
Beginner

Finished Size
Quilt Size: 53" x 73"
Block Size: 6" x 12"
Number of Blocks: 13

Materials
- ⅛ yard dark teal No. 2 batik
- ⅓ yard each dark teal No. 1 batik, light teal No. 1 batik and light teal No. 2 batik
- 1 yard dark teal No. 3 batik
- 3 yards cream batik
- Backing to size
- Batting to size
- Thread
- Basic sewing tools and supplies

Project Notes
Read all instructions before beginning this project.

Stitch right sides together using a ¼" seam allowance unless otherwise specified.

Materials and cutting lists assume 40" of usable fabric width for yardage.

Foundations
6" x 12" Finished Block
Make 13

Cutting

From dark teal No. 2 batik:
- Cut 1 (2½" by fabric width) strip.
  Subcut strip into 2 each 2½" x 6½" C and 2½" x 8½" B strips.

From dark teal No. 1 batik:
- Cut 3 (2½" by fabric width) strips.
  Subcut strips into 6 each 2½" x 6½" C and 2½" x 8½" B strips.

From light teal No. 1 batik:
- Cut 3 (2½" by fabric width) strips.
  Subcut strips into 6 each 2½" x 6½" C and 2½" x 8½" B strips.

From light teal No. 2 batik:
- Cut 3 (2½" by fabric width) strips.
  Subcut strips into 6 each 2½" x 6½" C and 2½" x 8½" B strips.

From dark teal No. 3 batik:

- Cut 3 (2½" by fabric width) strips.
  Subcut strips into 6 each 2½" x 6½" C
  and 2½" x 8½" B strips.
- Cut 7 (2¼" by fabric width) binding strips.

From cream batik:

- Cut 4 (13" by fabric width) strips.
  Subcut strips into 4 (13" x 22") F, 2 (7" x 10½") D
  and 13 (2½" x 8½") A rectangles.
- Cut 1 (48½" by fabric width) strip.
  Subcut strip lengthwise into 2 (16" x 48½")
  G strips and 3 (2½" x 48½") E strips.

Completing the Blocks

1. To make one block, select two each same-fabric B
and C strips and one A rectangle.

2. Sew B strips to opposite sides of the A rectangle
as shown in Figure 1 to make an A-B unit; press.

Figure 1   **Figure 2**

3. Referring to Figure 2, sew C strips on the top and
bottom of the A-B unit to make one Foundations
block; press.

4. Repeat steps 1–3 to make a total of 13
Foundations blocks as shown in Figure 3.

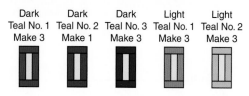

Dark Teal No. 1 Make 3 Dark Teal No. 2 Make 1 Dark Teal No. 3 Make 3 Light Teal No. 1 Make 3 Light Teal No. 2 Make 3

Figure 3

Completing the Quilt

1. Referring to Figure 4, arrange blocks from top to
bottom and stitch into three vertical rows as follows:

Row 1: dark teal No. 1, light teal No. 2, dark teal No. 3
and light teal No. 1

Row 2: dark teal No. 2, light teal No. 1, dark teal No. 1,
light teal No. 2 and dark teal No. 3

Row 3: light teal No. 2, dark teal No. 3, light teal No. 1
and dark teal No. 1

Row 1   Row 2   Row 3

Figure 4

2. Press each row and label.

3. Join E strips on the short ends to make one long
strip. Subcut strip into two 2½" x 60½" E strips.

4. Sew E strips on opposite sides of Row 2 as shown
in Figure 5; press. Sew D rectangles to the top and
bottom to complete the center unit; press.

Center Unit

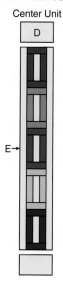

D

E→

Figure 5

5. Referring to Figure 6, sew a G strip on the left side of Row 1; press. Sew an F rectangle to the top and bottom to complete the left unit; press.

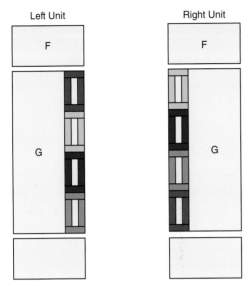

Figure 6   Figure 7

6. Sew a G strip to the right side of Row 3 as shown in Figure 7; press. Sew an F rectangle to the top and bottom to complete the right unit; press.

7. Referring to the Assembly Diagram, arrange and sew the left, center and right units together to complete the quilt top; press.

8. Layer, quilt as desired and bind referring to Quilting Basics on page 47. Sample quilt was machine-quilted with an edge-to-edge feather swirl pattern. ●

Foundations
Assembly Diagram 53" x 73"

Inspiration

"Charitable sewing is incredibly important and satisfying. Using your skills and knowledge to support vital causes or to bring happiness to others is a great way to pay it back and pay it forward. This quilt was fun to make, and I know it will find a good home through the Ovarian Cancer Association. Thank you for allowing me to be part of this charity quilting book!" —Lyn Brown

This is the perfect pattern to show-case a themed fabric, be it for a charity or a special interest.

Sticks in a Stack

This quilt is easy to make and is suitable for cancer patients, nursing home residents or those who are grieving. It's also a great choice to use leftover 2½" strips for a quilt to complement any home.

Designed & Quilted by Holly Daniels

Skill Level
Beginner

Finished Size
Quilt Size: 54" x 58"

Materials
- Scraps of brown, gold, rust and turquoise tonals, solids and prints to total approximately 1 yard
- 1⅓ yards medium tan print
- 2½ yards cream tonal
- Backing to size
- Batting to size
- Thread
- Basic sewing tools and supplies

Project Notes
Read all instructions before beginning this project.

Stitch right sides together using a ¼" seam allowance unless otherwise specified.

Materials and cutting lists assume 40" of usable fabric width for yardage.

Cutting

From scraps:
- Cut 36 (2½" x 8½") C rectangles.

From medium tan print:
- Cut 3 (2½" by fabric width) A strips.
- Cut 6 (2½" by fabric width) F strips.
- Cut 6 (2¼" by fabric width) binding strips.

From cream tonal:
- Cut 6 (2½" by fabric width) B strips.
- Cut 3 (14½" by fabric width) strips.
  Subcut strips into 39 (2½" x 14½") D strips.
- Cut 8 (2½" by fabric width) E strips.

Completing the Quilt

1. Arrange and stitch a B strip on each side of an A strip along length to make a B-A-B strip set as shown in Figure 1; press. Repeat to make a total of three B-A-B strip sets. Subcut strip sets into 36 (2½" x 6½") B-A-B units.

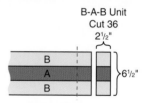

Figure 1

2. Referring to Figure 2, sew a C strip to a short end of a B-A-B unit to make an A-B-C unit; press. Repeat to make a total of 36 A-B-C units.

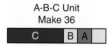

Figure 2

3. Referring to the Assembly Diagram for orientation of A-B-C units, alternately stitch 13 D strips and 12 A-B-C units into a vertical row; press. Repeat to make a total of three vertical rows.

4. Join E strips on the short ends to make one long strip; press. Subcut strip into six 2½" x 50½" E strips.

5. Alternately stitch four E strips and vertical rows together, beginning and ending with an E strip, to make the quilt center; press.

6. Sew the two remaining E strips to the top and bottom of the quilt center; press.

7. Join F strips on the short ends to make one long strip; press. Subcut strip into four 2½" x 54½" F strips.

8. Sew F strips to opposite sides of the quilt center and to the top and bottom to complete the quilt top; press.

9. Layer, quilt as desired and bind referring to Quilting Basics on page 47. Sample quilt was machine-quilted in a freehand heart-and-loop allover pattern. ●

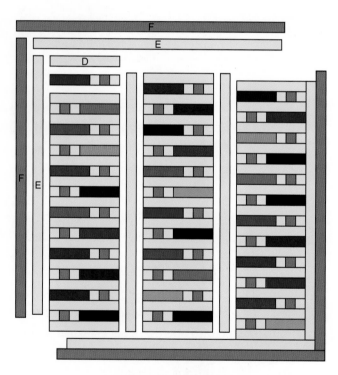

Sticks in a Stack
Assembly Diagram 54" x 58"

Inspiration

"I was inspired to create this quilt by a dear friend's loss of an adult daughter to a short illness. As a quilter, my first thought was to give her something soft and warm to comfort her." —Holly Daniels

Using a collection of your favorite colors in this easy pattern can change it from a great charity quilt to a stunning weekend project for yourself.

Charity Lines

Gather a group of creative friends for an evening of charity quilting. Knock out six quilts in a couple of hours. This versatile pattern is perfect for both charity and personal stitching.

Designed & Quilted by CJ Behling

Skill Level
Beginner

Finished Size
Quilt Size: 50" x 61½"

Materials
- ⅓ yard white tonal
- ½ yard each of 7 coordinating prints
- ⅝ yard dark blue tonal
- Backing to size
- Batting to size
- Thread
- Basic sewing tools and supplies

Project Notes
Read all instructions before beginning this project.

Stitch right sides together using a ¼" seam allowance unless otherwise specified.

Materials and cutting lists assume 40" of usable fabric width for yardage.

Cutting

From white tonal:
- Cut 2 (3½" by fabric width) strips.

From each coordinating print:
- Cut 2 (6½" by fabric width) strips.

From dark blue tonal:
- Cut 6 (2¼" by fabric width) binding strips.

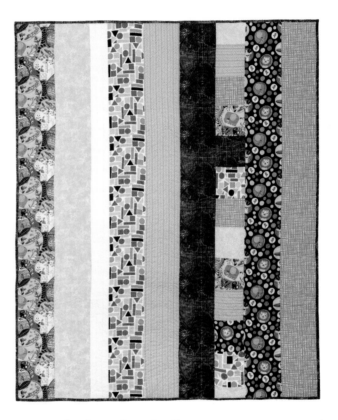

Completing the Quilt

1. Sew two same-fabric coordinating print strips together on the short ends to make one long strip; press. Subcut strip into one 6½" x 62" B strip and two 5½" C squares. Repeat with remaining coordinating print strips to make a total of seven 62" B strips and 14 C squares. **Note:** *Only 13 C squares are used in the quilt.*

2. Join white tonal strips on the short ends to make one long strip; press. Trim to make one 3½" x 62" A strip.

3. Arrange and stitch 13 C squares into a pieced row as shown in Figure 1; press. Trim pieced row to 62" length, removing excess from both ends.

Pieced Row

Figure 1

4. Referring to the Placement Diagram, arrange and stitch the pieced row and A and B strips on the long sides to complete the quilt top; press.

5. Layer, quilt as desired and bind referring to Quilting Basics on page 47. Sample quilt was machine-quilted with straight-line stitching. ●

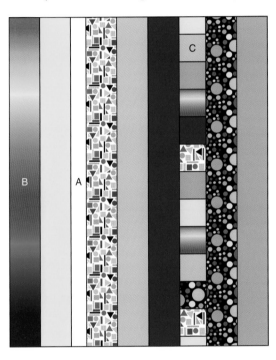

Charity Lines
Placement Diagram 50" x 61¹⁄₂"

Inspiration

"I believe that when God gives you a talent, he intends you to use it to help others, and when you do, what you receive in return is exquisite and priceless. My quilts from this book will be going to my local police department. Operation Wrap is a new project I am spearheading to place quilts in the hands of children in traumatic situations for warmth and comfort. I encourage others to do the same." —CJ Behling

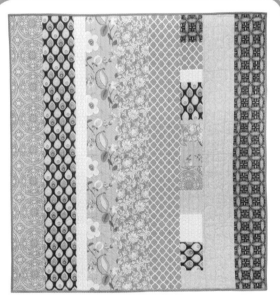

This is the perfect pattern to use with get-together groups sewing for any cause or maybe for any young child in need of a quilt. Simply change your fabrics to meet your needs.

Memories Fidget Quilt

Various tactile "fidget items" were incorporated into this weighted quilt. It was designed for Alzheimer's patients to keep their hands busy, but it can also be used by people with autism.

Designed & Quilted by Nancy Walhout Recker

Skill Level
Confident Beginner

Finished Size
Quilt Size: 51" x 51"
Block Size: 9" x 9"
Number of Blocks: 20

Materials
- Large scraps for zipper lining pieces
- ⅜ yard orange tonal
- ⅝ yard light blue solid
- ⅞ yard lime green tonal
- 1 yard total assorted medium pink tonals
- 3¾ yards dark pink tonal
- 5 yards flannel
- 3–5 pounds of polyester weighted stuffing pellets
- 4 (9") zippers: green, pink, light blue and orange
- Fidget items: fabric scraps, beads, buttons, rickrack, ribbons, fringe, shoelaces, textured fabrics, cord, cord locks, elastic, plastic rings, washers and keys
- Thread
- Basic sewing tools and supplies

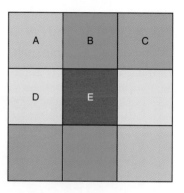

Nine-Patch
9" x 9" Finished Block
Make 12

Stripe
9" x 9" Finished Block
Make 8

Project Notes
Read all instructions before beginning this project.

Stitch right sides together using a ¼" seam allowance unless otherwise specified.

Materials and cutting lists assume 40" of usable fabric width for yardage.

Cutting

From large scraps:
- Cut 4 (5" x 12") M rectangles.

From orange tonal:
- Cut 6 (1⅜" by fabric width) G strips.

From light blue solid:
- Cut 4 (3½" by fabric width) D strips.
- Cut 3 (1¾" by fabric width) J strips.
- Cut 1 (2" by fabric width) strip.
  Subcut strip into 8 (2" x 3") K rectangles.

From lime green tonal:
- Cut 3 (3½" by fabric width) B strips.
- Cut 6 (2" by fabric width) F strips.

From medium pink tonals:
- Cut 3 (3½" by fabric width) A strips.
- Cut 3 (3½" by fabric width) C strips.
- Cut 6 (1⅜" by fabric width) I strips.

From dark pink tonal:
- Cut 2 (3½" by fabric length) strips.
  Subcut strips into 1 (3½" x 51½") O strip,
      2 (3½" x 40") E strips, 2 (3½" x 45½") N strips
      and 1 (3½" x 5½") L rectangle.
- Cut 2 (1⅛" by fabric length) strips.
  Subcut strips into 6 (1⅛" x 40") H strips.
- Cut 2 (61" by remaining fabric width) strips
  for backing.

From flannel:
- Cut 3 (58" by fabric width) strips.

Completing the Blocks & Units

1. Arrange and stitch together one each A, B and C strip on the long edges to make an A-B-C strip set as shown in Figure 1; press. Repeat to make a total of three A-B-C strip sets. Subcut strip sets into 26 (3½" x 9½") A-B-C units.

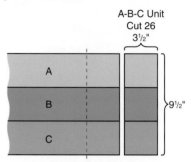

Figure 1

2. Referring to Figure 2, arrange and stitch two D strips on opposite long sides of an E strip to make a D-E strip set; press. Repeat to make a second D-E strip set. Subcut strip sets into 13 (3½" x 9½") D-E units.

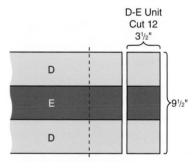

Figure 2

3. Arrange two A-B-C units on opposite sides of a D-E unit as shown in Figure 3. Stitch units together to complete one Nine-Patch block; press. Repeat to make a total of 12 blocks.

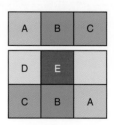

Figure 3

4. Referring to Figure 4, fold an L rectangle in half, wrong sides together, to make a 2¾" x 3½" pocket piece; press.

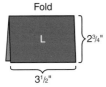

Figure 4

5. Remove stitching from the remaining D-E unit and position the pocket piece on the right side of the E square, aligning raw edges on the sides and bottom as shown in Figure 5; baste in place.

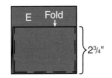

Figure 5

6. Referring to Figure 6, fold an 8" length of ribbon in half and thread the fold about an inch through a key, making a loop. Put the tails of the ribbon through the loop and pull tightly to attach the key securely. Baste the loose ends of the ribbon to the top center of the E square.

Figure 6

7. Stitch the D-E unit back together, being careful not to stitch through the loose section of the ribbon as shown in Figure 7; press.

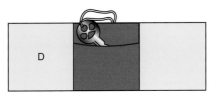

Figure 7

8. Referring to Figure 8, arrange and stitch the two remaining A-B-C units on opposite sides of the D-E unit from step 7 to make one key unit; press.

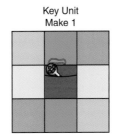

Key Unit
Make 1

Figure 8

9. Arrange and stitch two each F, G, H and I strips and one J strip lengthwise together as shown in Figure 9 to make a strip set; press. Repeat to make a total of three strip sets. Subcut strip sets into eight 9½" x 9½" Stripe blocks and four 9½" x 9½" zipper segments.

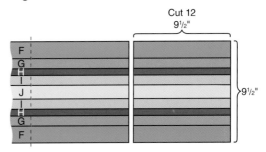

Figure 9

10. Referring to Figure 10, fold a K rectangle in half with wrong sides together. Repeat with a second K rectangle.

Figure 10

11. Baste a K rectangle to each end of a 9" zipper, placing the folded edges at the zipper stays as shown in Figure 11.

Figure 11

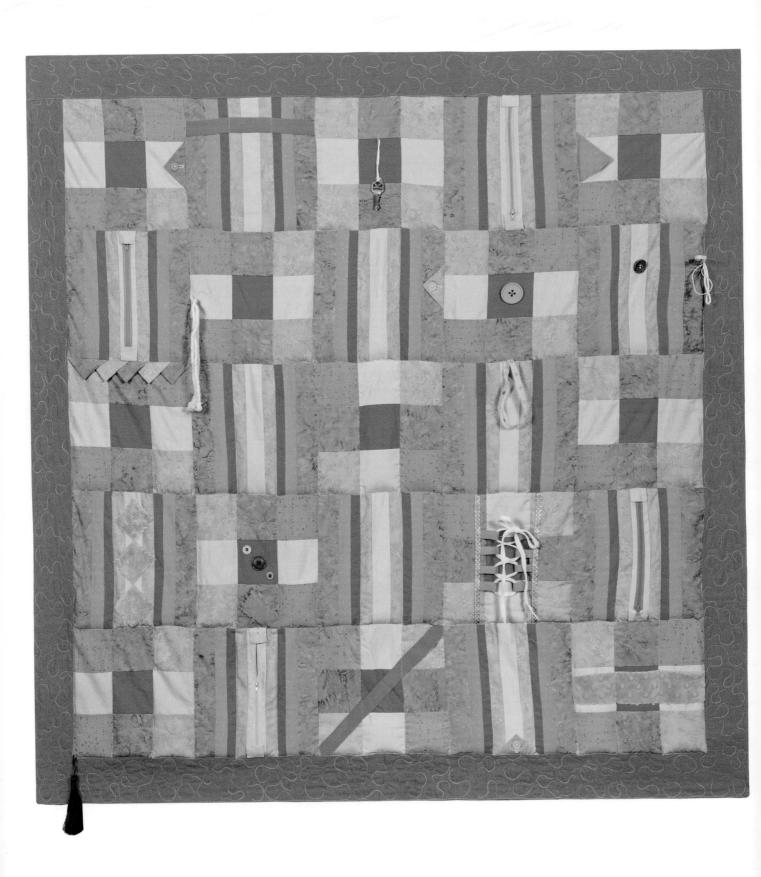

12. Referring to Figure 12, cut a zipper segment in half along the center of the J strip to make two sections.

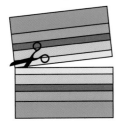

Figure 12

13. Center and sew the zipper to the cut edge of one section, right sides together, as shown in Figure 13; press the section open. Repeat to stitch the zipper to the cut edge of the second section. Trim zipper ends even; topstitch along edges of fabric to hold in place. Trim unit to 9½" x 9½", if needed.

Figure 13

14. Referring to Figure 14, center M rectangle right side up behind zipper for lining. Baste in place. Trim edges even with top piece to complete one zipper unit.

Zipper Unit
Make 4

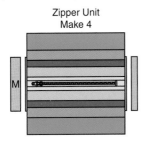

Figure 14

15. Repeat steps 10–14 to make a total of four zipper units.

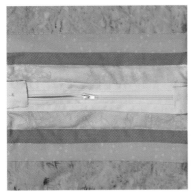

Adding the Optional Fidget Items

Any combination of fidget items can be added to the blocks before assembly.

Prairie Points

1. Cut desired number of 3½" x 3½" squares from fabric scraps. Fold each square in half diagonally to form a triangle, wrong sides together. Fold in half again, matching raw edges; press to make prairie points. Add a buttonhole in each point, if desired.

2. Referring to Figure 15, baste raw edge of a prairie point or several prairie points to the raw edge of any block, tucking one point into the previous point to fit block edge. If using buttonholes, sew a button under the prairie point.

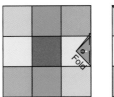

Figure 15

Textured Fabrics

1. Add a non-fraying textured fabric piece to any block by cutting desired shape, placing on the block and topstitching around the edges to hold, as shown in Figure 16.

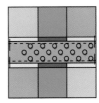

Figure 16

2. To add loose textured fidgets, stitch long edges of a 5½" x 9½" textured fabric strip together, right sides facing, to make a tube. Turn tube right side out and press with seam centered in the back. Position tube across any block, matching raw edges on opposite sides. Baste raw edges to hold.

3. Fold a 3" x 6" textured fabric scrap right sides together lengthwise. Stitch long side. Turn right side out; press. Fold in half to make a loop. Baste to side of any block, aligning raw edges.

Button Fasteners & Lacing

1. Cut 8 (2½") ribbon pieces; fold in half to make loops. Baste raw ends of four loops in a row 2½" from one side edge of any block as shown in Figure 17. Repeat with remaining four loops on opposite side. Cover raw edges with ribbon or trim; stitch in place. Thread a shoelace through the loops and tie a bow at the top. Tack the shoelace at the bottom to secure.

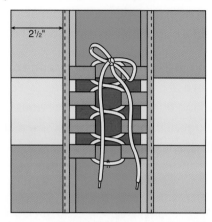

Figure 17

2. Fold a 4"–6" length of elastic, cord or ribbon in half; baste the two raw ends to a raw edge of any block. Sew buttons under loops.

3. String plastic beads, washers or rings on an 8"–10" piece of elastic, cord or ribbon. Repeat step 2 to attach to a block.

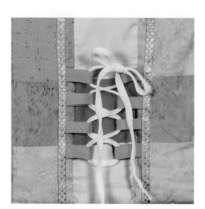

Rickrack, Fringe & Other Trims

1. Cut 3 (12") lengths of medium cord; baste one end of each at the edge of any block. Tie a knot in the loose end of each cord (Figure 18). Braid ends together, if desired.

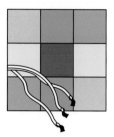

Figure 18

2. Baste jumbo rickrack, fringe or pompom trims with bound edges along the edges of any block; sew into the seams when blocks are joined.

3. Insert tassel cords into seams.

4. Stitch trims with different textures flat in parallel rows.

5. Add buttons of varying sizes and colors individually or in groups.

Pockets

1. Refer to steps 4–6 in Completing the Blocks & Units to insert pockets when piecing a block.

2. To add a pocket to a completed block, cut one 3½" or smaller scrap fabric square and one matching-size scrap lining square. Stitch around squares, with right sides together, leaving a small opening for turning. Turn right side out; press. Turn opening edges in and slip-stitch closed. Topstitch to any block, leaving top edge open.

Completing the Quilt

1. Referring to Figure 19 (below), arrange the Nine-Patch and Stripe blocks and key and zipper units into five rows. Sew into rows, being careful not to sew through fidget items. Sew rows together to complete the quilt center; press.

2. Sew N borders to opposite sides of the quilt and the O border to the bottom to complete the quilt top; press.

3. Sew backing strips together along length with a ½" seam allowance; press seam open. Trim to make the 54" x 61" backing piece.

4. Sew flannel strips together on long sides with a ½" seam allowance; press seams open. Topstitch seam allowance edges to hold in place. Cut into two 54" x 58" insert pieces.

5. Layer two flannel inserts with right sides together; add the backing rectangle, right side up, aligning the long side and bottom edges, and leaving the backing extending at the top edge. Add the quilt top, wrong side up, centered 2" above the bottom edges of the backing and flannel pieces as shown in Figure 20.

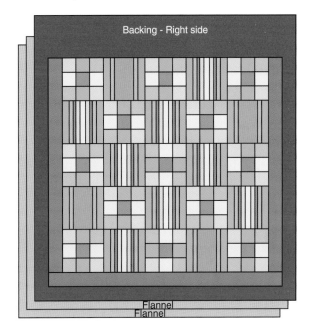

Figure 20

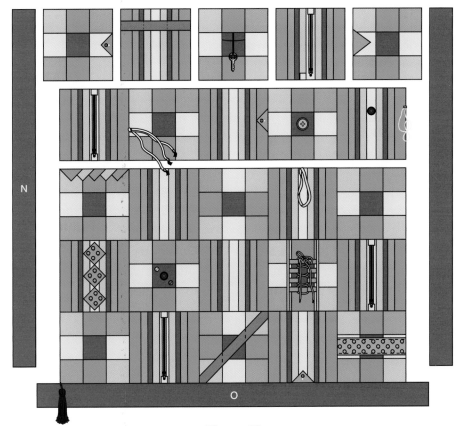

Figure 19

6. Stitch side and bottom edges together ¼" inside the quilt top edges, leaving the top open. Trim side and bottom edges even with the quilt top. Trim flannel and backing side edges above the quilt top ½" wider than quilt top at each edge. Turn right side out with the flannel sandwiched between the quilt top and backing. Press and topstitch ⅛" from side and bottom edges to hold in place.

7. Referring to Figure 21, stitch in the ditch of the bottom border seam. Starting at the top of the bottom border, stitch in the ditch from bottom to top every 3" to make a total of 15 channels for the weighted pellets. Do not stitch over fidget items.

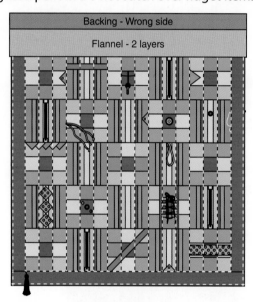

Figure 21

8. Decide if you want to stitch the channels closed across the quilt every 3" or 9". There will be 225 pockets if sewn every 3" and 75 pockets if sewn every 9".

9. Find the total weight (in ounces) of the pellets and divide that number by the number of pockets. This will be the approximate weight of pellets that go in each pocket.

10. Pour the calculated amount of pellets into each of the channels between the two flannel layers, being sure the pellets reach the bottom of the channel. *Note: A funnel or long tube is useful to help pour.*

11. Stitch in the ditch from side border to opposite side border at either the predetermined 3" or 9" interval to close in the pellets.

12. Repeat steps 10 and 11 until all pockets have been filled and have reached the top of the quilt. Stitch the quilt closed through all layers, ¼" from the top of the quilt.

13. Trim flannel inserts to 2¾" above top of quilt and backing to 6½" above top of quilt. Fold flannel side edges in ½" on each edge; press. Fold side edges of backing over edges of flannel; press. Press top raw edge of backing under ½".

14. Fold backing in half and fold over flannel and ¼" over top edge of quilt top to form a 3" top border and to hide the channel-closing stitches as shown in Figure 22. Topstitch closed along edge of quilt top. Topstitch ⅛" from side and top edges of border.

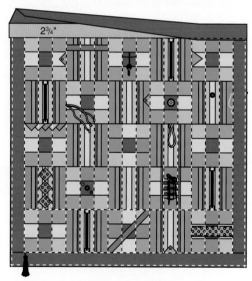

Figure 22

15. Quilt outer border to add texture, if desired. Sample quilt was machine-quilted with a free-motion meander. ●

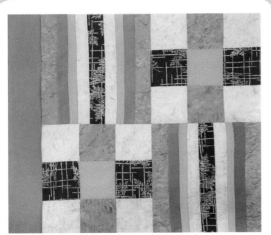

Don't forget to consider this pattern when you need a great weekend project. To make it an everyday quilt simply leave off the "extras" and only do the blocks. Any color group will work nicely with this layout.

Inspiration

"This quilt was made for a special friend who has Alzheimer's disease. If people would like to find a place in need of these quilts to donate, most senior centers would love to have them." —Nancy Walhout Recker

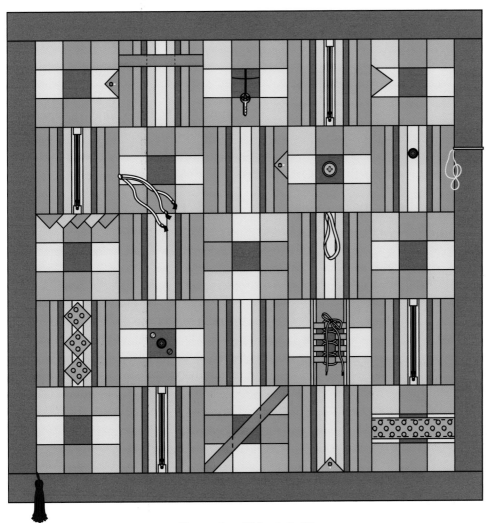

Memories Fidget Quilt
Placement Diagram 51" x 51"

Seat Belt Pillow

This little pillow can be made in a short time, but it will bring lots of comfort to any patient with a port or who has had a mastectomy. It's designed to fit on any seat belt.

Design by Carolyn S. Vagts

Skill Level
Beginner

Finished Size
Pillow Size: 15" x 7" before stuffing

Materials
- 2 fat quarters of coordinating blue prints
- 18" square batting
- Polyester fiberfill
- 6" hook-and-loop tape
- Thread
- Basic sewing tools and supplies

Project Notes
Read all instructions before beginning this project.

Stitch right sides together using a ¼" seam allowance unless otherwise specified.

Materials and cutting lists assume 20" of usable fabric width for fat quarters.

Cutting
Designate one fat quarter for the pillow top and one for the pillow bottom.

From each fat quarter:
- Cut 1 (7½" x 15½") A rectangle.

From top fat quarter:
- Cut 3 (3½" x 9") B strips.

From batting:
- Cut 2 (7½" x 15½") rectangles.

Completing the Pillow

1. Layer the batting rectangles between the A rectangles with right sides toward batting as shown in Figure 1.

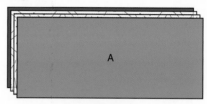

Figure 1

2. Referring to Figure 2, stitch around the layered batting and fabric, leaving a 3" opening in the center of both long sides.

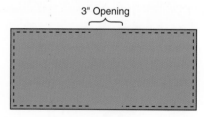

Figure 2

3. Clip corners and turn the unit right side out through one of the openings; press.

4. Stitch across pillow cover 2" from each long side as shown in Figure 3.

Figure 3

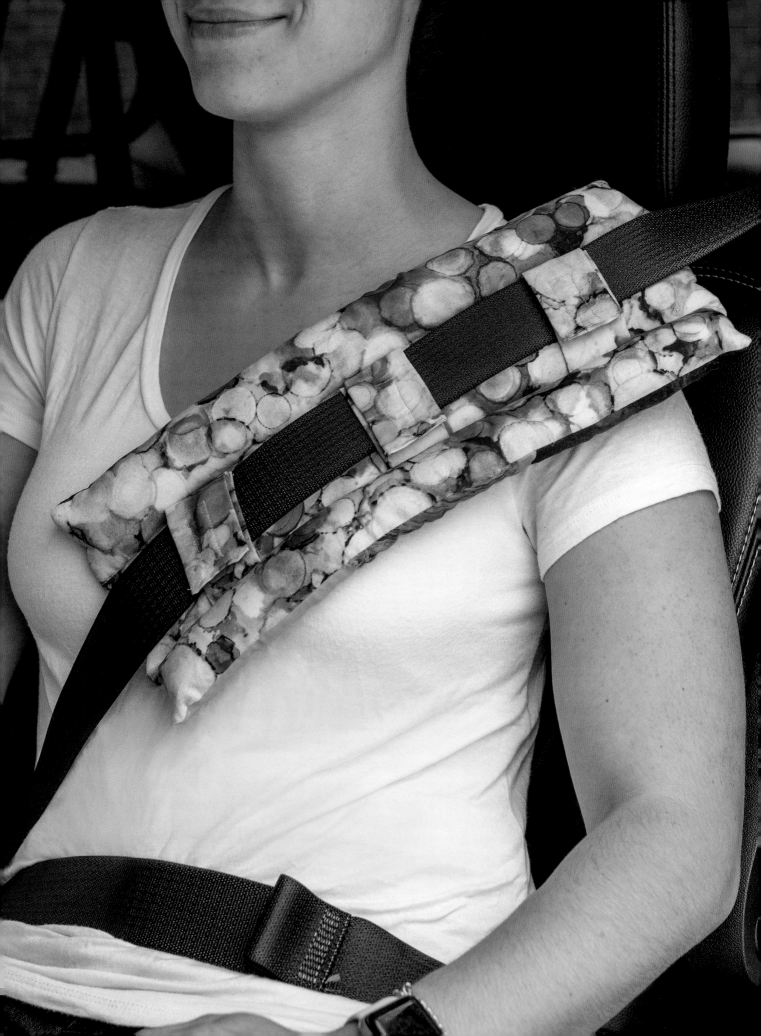

5. Referring to Figure 4, fold a B strip in half lengthwise with right sides together and stitch one short end and down the long side leaving one end open.

Figure 4

6. Turn right side out and press under ¼" on the open end; stitch end closed to make a fastening band.

7. Repeat steps 5 and 6 to make a total of three fastening bands.

8. Position the three fastening bands on the pillow cover top as shown in Figure 5, spacing bands equally; stitch into place on the 2" stitching lines.

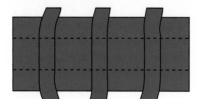

Figure 5

9. Stuff each 2" channel on the long sides of the pillow cover with polyester fiberfill and slip-stitch openings closed.

10. Cut the hook-and-loop tape into three equal pieces; machine-stitch the hook piece to the inside of one end of each fastener band and the loop piece to the outside of the other end to complete the pillow. ●

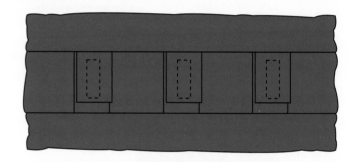

Seat Belt Pillow
Placement Diagram 15" x 7" before stuffing

Inspiration

"I wish I had made one of these several years ago when my own son went through a serious illness. It would have been a great source of comfort while traveling back and forth to the hospital."
—Carolyn S. Vagts

Pillowcases for Causes

This pillowcase can be made in less than an hour. It's easy and can be made for just about any charity since fabrics can be themed to make it work for any cause. Once you make one, you'll want to make them for all your friends and family members.

Design by Carolyn S. Vagts

Skill Level
Beginner

Finished Size
Pillowcase Size: 31½" x 20½"

Materials
- ⅛ yard black solid
- ½ yard lime green solid
- ⅞ yard novelty print
- Thread
- Basic sewing tools and supplies

Project Notes
Read all instructions before beginning this project.

Stitch right sides together using a ¼" seam allowance unless otherwise specified.

Materials and cutting lists assume 42" of usable fabric width for yardage.

Cutting

From black solid:
- Cut 1 (2" by fabric width) C strip.

From lime green solid:
- Cut 1 (11" by fabric width) B strip.

From novelty print:
- Cut 1 (27" by fabric width) A rectangle.

Completing the Pillowcase

1. Press the C strip in half lengthwise with wrong sides together as shown in Figure 1.

Figure 1

2. Referring to Figure 2, position the folded C strip on the right side of B, aligning raw edges on the long side.

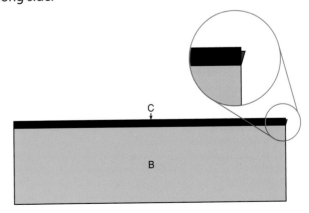

Figure 2

3. Arrange A rectangle, right side down, on top of C and B as shown in Figure 3 aligning the raw edges; pin in place.

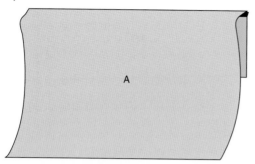

Figure 3

4. Referring to Figure 4, roll up the A rectangle until it is small enough to bring the B rectangle around it and pin to the top of the stack, aligning raw edges. Stitch along the raw edges through all layers; do not catch the rolled section in the stitching.

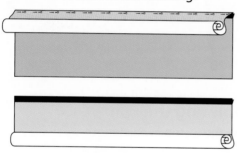

Figure 4

5. Pull the rolled A rectangle out through one end of the stitched tube and press flat, pressing C toward B.

6. Fold the unit in half with wrong sides together as shown in Figure 5, matching sides and bottom edges; press.

Figure 5

7. Using a scant ¼" seam allowance, stitch along the side and bottom edges.

8. Referring to Figure 6, turn pillowcase wrong side out; press side and bottom seams flat. Stitch again with a generous ¼" seam allowance, enclosing the previous seam to make a French seam. Turn right side out; re-press edges to complete one pillowcase. ●

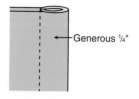

←Generous ¼"

Figure 6

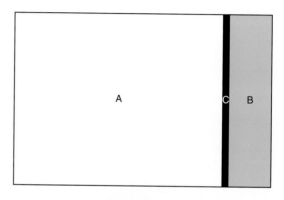

Pillowcases for Causes
Placement Diagram 31½" x 20½"

Color coordinate your pillowcases for kids or grandkids. This pillowcase can easily be made for any occasion.

Chemo Scarf

By choosing to use batiks, this scarf can be both stylish and easy. There is no need to worry about the right or wrong side. You can make two with only 1 yard of fabric.

Design by Carolyn S. Vagts

Skill Level
Beginner

Finished Size
Scarf Size: 42" x 21"

Materials
- 1⅛ yards plum batik
- 3½" x 20" strip batting
- Thread
- Basic sewing tools and supplies

Project Notes
Read all instructions before beginning this project.

Stitch right sides together using a ¼" seam allowance unless otherwise specified.

Materials and cutting lists assume 40" of usable fabric width for yardage.

Cutting

From plum batik:
- Cut 1 (36") square.
  Subcut square in half on 1 diagonal to make 2 A triangles.

Completing the Scarf
1. Press under ⅛" on both short sides of one A triangle. Press under ¼" and stitch on inner fold to hem both short sides as shown in Figure 1.

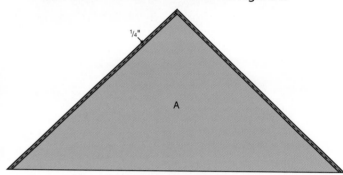

Figure 1

2. Referring to Figure 2, press a ½" fold on the long side of A. Center and firmly tuck the batting under the fold.

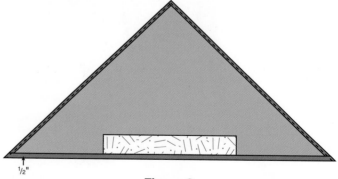

Figure 2

3. Fold the batting and fabric over to create a 3½" band; pin in place. Trim both ends of the band, leaving a ¼" seam allowance at each end as shown in Figure 3. Fold and tuck the seam allowance into the band.

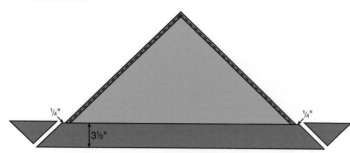

Figure 3

4. Referring to Figure 4, topstitch one end of the band closed, continue to stitch along the long open side of the band and down the opposite end.

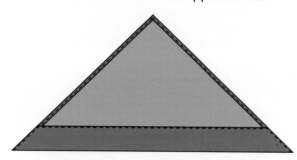

Figure 4

5. Stitching through all layers, secure the opposite short ends of the batting as shown in Figure 5. Stitch horizontal lines 1" apart in the batted section to hold batting in place and prevent bias stretch of the fabric.

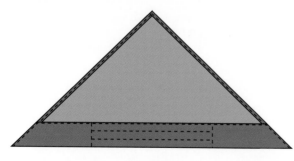

Figure 5

6. Repeat steps 1–5 to complete a second scarf, if desired.

7. Referring to Figure 6, tie the scarf in place as follows:

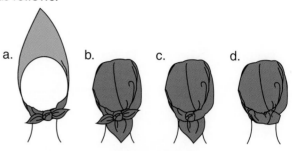

Figure 6

a. Tie the two long points together at the back of the neck.

b. Bring the middle point down and under the knot.

c. Tuck the knot ends under the knot.

d. Bring the middle point up and over the knot and tuck in to create a "bun" at the nape of the neck. ●

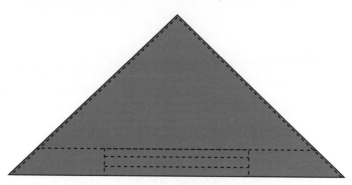

Chemo Scarf
Placement Diagram 42" x 21"

Inspiration

"I've had several friends who have lost their hair during treatment. It's a hard time for anyone when this happens, and if a bright, lovely chemo scarf can bring a ray of sunshine to their day, it's a good thing." —Carolyn S. Vagts

Quilting Basics

The following is a reference guide. For more information, consult a comprehensive quilting book.

Quilt Backing & Batting

We suggest that you cut your backing and batting 8" larger than the finished quilt-top size. If preparing the backing from standard-width fabrics, remove the selvages and sew two or three lengths together; press seams open. If using 108"-wide fabric, trim to size on the straight grain of the fabric.

Prepare batting the same size as your backing. You can purchase prepackaged sizes or battings by the yard and trim to size.

Quilting

1. Press quilt top on both sides and trim all loose threads.

2. Make a quilt sandwich by layering the backing right side down, batting and quilt top centered right side up on flat surface and smooth out. Pin or baste layers together to hold.

3. Mark quilting design on quilt top and quilt as desired by hand or machine. **Note:** *If you are sending your quilt to a professional quilter, contact them for specifics about preparing your quilt for quilting.*

4. When quilting is complete, remove pins or basting. Trim batting and backing edges even with raw edges of quilt top.

Binding the Quilt

1. Join binding strips on short ends with diagonal seams to make one long strip; trim seams to ¼" and press seams open (Figure A).

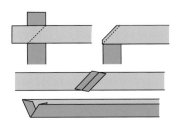

Figure A

2. Fold 1" of one short end to wrong side and press. Fold the binding strip in half with wrong sides together along length, again referring to Figure A; press.

3. Starting about 3" from the folded short end, sew binding to quilt top edges, matching raw edges and using a ¼" seam. Stop stitching ¼" from corner and backstitch (Figure B).

Stop ¼"

Figure B

4. Fold binding up at a 45-degree angle to seam and then down even with quilt edges, forming a pleat at corner, referring to Figure C.

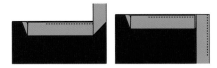

Figure C

5. Resume stitching from corner edge as shown in Figure C, down quilt side, backstitching ¼" from next corner. Repeat, mitering all corners, stitching to within 3" of starting point.

6. Trim binding end long enough to tuck inside starting end and complete stitching (Figure D).

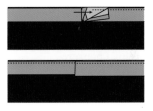

Figure D

7. Fold binding to quilt back and stitch in place by hand or machine to complete your quilt.

Special Thanks

Please join us in thanking the talented designers whose work is featured in this collection.

CJ Behling
Charity Lines, page 25

Lyn Brown
Foundations, page 19

Holly Daniels
Patriotic Star, page 10
Sticks in a Stack, page 22

Karen DuMont of KariePatch Designs
Sassy Sally, page 14
Simple Simon, page 3

Nancy Walhout Recker
Memories Fidget Quilt, page 28

Carolyn S. Vagts
Chemo Scarf, page 44
Neo-Preemie Quilt, page 6
Pillowcases for Causes, page 41
Seat Belt Pillow, page 38

Supplies

We would like to thank the following manufacturers who provided materials to our designers to make sample projects for this book.

Neo-Preemie Quilt, page 6: Ahoy collection by Gingiber for Moda Fabrics

Patriotic Star, page 10: Warm & White batting from The Warm Company

Foundations, page 19: Batiks from Hoffman California International

Sticks in a Stack, page 22: Soft & Bright batting from The Warm Company

Published by Annie's, 306 East Parr Road, Berne, IN 46711. Printed in USA. Copyright © 2018 Annie's. All rights reserved. This publication may not be reproduced in part or in whole without written permission from the publisher.

RETAIL STORES: If you would like to carry this publication or any other Annie's publications, visit AnniesWSL.com.

Every effort has been made to ensure that the instructions in this publication are complete and accurate. We cannot, however, take responsibility for human error, typographical mistakes or variations in individual work. Please visit AnniesCustomerService.com to check for pattern updates.

ISBN: 978-1-59012-932-6

1 2 3 4 5 6 7 8 9